To: _____

From: _____

Date: _____

i will GIVE THANKS

90 Days to a More Grateful Heart

Becky Shannon

ZONDERVAN

I Will Give Thanks

© 2024 Becky Shannon

Requests for information should be addressed to customercare@harpercollins.com.

Published in Grand Rapids, Michigan, by Zondervan. Zondervan is a registered trademark of The Zondervan Corporation, L.L.C., a wholly owned subsidiary of HarperCollins Christian Publishing, Inc.

ISBN 978-0-310-46427-3 (audiobook)
ISBN 978-0-310-46423-5 (eBook)
ISBN 978-0-310-46425-9 (HC)

Art: Becky Shannon
Art direction: Tiffany Forrester
Interior design: Mallory Collins

Printed in Malaysia

24 25 26 27 28 OFF 10 9 8 7 6 5 4 3 2 1

This book is dedicated to my Lord, Redeemer, and Friend, Jesus Christ. Without Him, this book would not have been written. I am so thankful for the freedom and peace His presence has breathed into my life and family. Thank You, Jesus!

Contents

give THANKS to the LORD, for HE IS GOOD; His love endures forever

1 Chronicles 16:34

Introduction
A Grateful Heart

Give thanks to the LORD, for he is good; his love endures forever.
1 CHRONICLES 16:34

Picture this: Your home is decorated all nice and cozy. There's a wonderful aroma in the air of a delicious dinner and a fresh-baked pie. You sit down with friends and family, soaking in the abundance. Your heart is so happy in this moment.

Fast-forward a few months, and everything feels like it's going wrong. You endure hit after hit on your marriage, your health, and your plans. You know you should still be thankful to God, but all you want to do is cry, "Why is this happening to me?"

Does this sound familiar? I know things can be difficult. You're doing your best and wondering why it feels as if you're getting punished for it. You try to keep a positive mindset through it all, but quite frankly, you're exhausted.

My hope is that through reading this book, you will feel strengthened and encouraged in the Lord. Over ninety days, I hope to not only grow your perspective on what a grateful heart can do in your life, but also grow your perspective on what *God* can do . . . and what He has done for you already.

A grateful heart is not simply a heart that says *thank you*. It is a heart that recognizes and believes in the goodness of God.

1

Taking Off the Blindfold

Taste and see that the LORD is good; blessed is the one who takes refuge in him.
PSALM 34:8

Way too early in the morning, before my alarm was set to go off, I heard my kids arguing in the hallway. How did they not know how to whisper?

I got up and grumbled my way to where they were, telling them to be quiet before they woke the baby. I barked orders for the older one to let the dog out, then told his sister she needed to unload the dishwasher. Their faces fell.

As I turned around to make some coffee, I saw that coffee had already been poured into my favorite mug, and a plate of eggs and toast was sitting next to it. Lying beside the plate was a note that read, "To Mom. Have a good day. ☺"

Remorse hit me. I had been so blinded by my frustration that I hadn't noticed they had been arguing over telling me about the surprise.

I quickly went to find them and apologize. We shared the coffee they had made me, and I made them some pancakes as a "thank you."

Have you ever been so stressed out that you forgot to look for the beautiful gifts God placed right in front of you? Having a grateful heart is a choice we make each day. In choosing gratitude, we take off our "blindfolds" and actively seek the blessings God gives us.

taste & SEE THAT the LORD IS GOOD.

psalm 34:8

IS YOUR HEART
gratefully in tune

WITH WHO GOD IS
and what He has done
IN YOUR LIFE?

2

Evidence of Growth

The fruit of the Spirit is love, joy, peace, forbearance, kindness, goodness,
faithfulness, gentleness and self-control. Against such things there is no law.
GALATIANS 5:22–23

Early on in life when I was reading through Scripture, the fruit of the Spirit listed in today's verses kept coming to mind. I looked them up and felt a little bit silly to realize that "thankfulness" was not one of them. So why did they keep coming to mind?

Gratitude and the fruit of the Spirit all grow from having a relationship with the Lord. When we know God, we become acutely aware of His goodness. Deep gratitude grows from realizing we don't deserve any of it.

A grateful heart has experienced God's unfailing love and is compelled to spread that love to others. It is filled with abundant joy. It remembers His words of promise and is at peace in times of chaos.

A grateful heart also sees God's patience, kindness, goodness, faithfulness, and self-control toward His children and strives to imitate His example.

My prayer for you today is that you take the time to assess your relationship with God. What is growing? What is thriving? Is your heart gratefully in tune with who God is and what He has done in your life?

3

A Gratitude Prayer

He predestined us to adoption as sons and daughters through Jesus
Christ to Himself, according to the good pleasure of His will.
EPHESIANS 1:5 NASB

Heavenly Father, I'm so grateful for Your perfect love.
*   You have chosen me and known me since before the foundations of*
the earth were laid.
*   Thank You for Your faithfulness and for never giving up on me.*
*   Thank You for calling me Your child.*
*   I love You, Lord!*
In Jesus' name, amen.

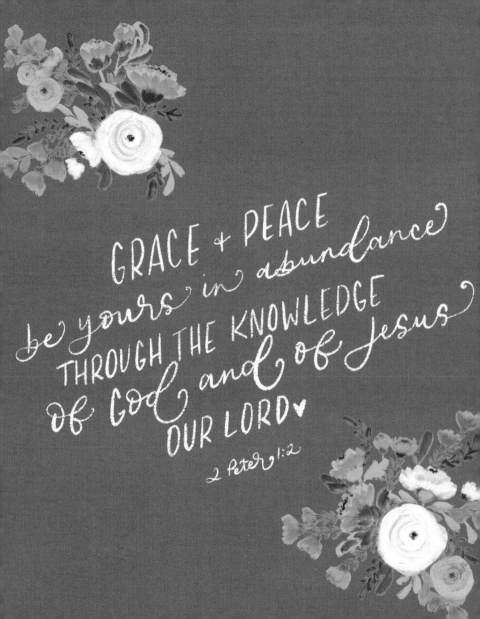

GRACE & PEACE
be yours in abundance
THROUGH THE KNOWLEDGE
of GOD and of Jesus
OUR LORD♥

2 Peter 1:2

4

Recognizing God

*Grace and peace be yours in abundance through the
knowledge of God and of Jesus our Lord.*

2 PETER 1:2

The Hebrew word for *gratitude* means to "recognize the good." I love that, because *who* is good all the time? *God* is. Every time we're reading the word *gratitude* in the Bible, we are literally being reminded to recognize God and His goodness.

But we cannot learn to recognize God if we do not have an intimate relationship with Him.

When we choose to know God, our relationship with Him grows, and our eyes become opened to who He is and what He's doing in our lives. By making the time to read His Word and to pray, we start to become transformed and have our minds renewed. The blindfold we once wore falls off, and we learn to recognize God and His goodness in both good and bad circumstances.

My hope for you today is that you take the first step toward getting to know God more intimately. May you experience His calming presence and unfailing love as you spend time reading His Word.

5

What Is Blinding You?

If we are faithless, he remains faithful, for he cannot disown himself.
2 TIMOTHY 2:13

I have called myself a Christian most of my life but have struggled with feeling thankful during difficult seasons. I have felt lost in the exhausting chaos of motherhood, the helplessness of watching loved ones struggling, and the overwhelming feeling of walking through everything alone.

In those times, my focus was usually on how bad I felt and how unfair things seemed. I would ask myself why I should even keep trying. What was the point? Where was God, and why did He hate me?

Looking back now, I can see God's hand in so many things. He has never left me. I was blinded by my anger, hurt, and selfishness and pushed myself further and further away from my relationship with Him. But even in my darkest days, God heard my cries for help and pulled me back to Him.

That is what God does. That is who God is. I am so thankful for His grace!

I encourage you today to think about what may be blinding you from seeing God's goodness in your life. Name it. Confess it. Give thanks to the Lord for His unfailing faithfulness and grace!

IF WE ARE
faithless, he
REMAINS FAITHFUL ·
for he cannot
DISOWN HIMSELF ♥

2 Timothy 2:13

REJOICE ALWAYS,
pray continually,
GIVE THANKS IN ALL
circumstances;
FOR THIS IS GOD'S WILL
FOR YOU IN
Christ Jesus

1 THESSALONIANS
5:16-18

6

Give Thanks in All Circumstances

Rejoice always, pray continually, give thanks in all circumstances;
for this is God's will for you in Christ Jesus.
1 THESSALONIANS 5:16–18

We've all thought it. How can we possibly be expected to say "thank you" for the loss, grief, fear, and pain we experience in life?

When my oldest son was diagnosed with type 1 diabetes, I struggled with seeing any good in the situation. No mama likes seeing her baby in the hospital, hooked up to an IV, giving himself shots, and relearning how to live.

When my son was released from the hospital, though, I was overflowing with gratitude. We had gotten help in time. He was doing well, and his doctors and nurses were wonderful. *Thank God!* Are things always perfect? No. But my son is still here with us, and for that, I will forever say, "Thank You, Lord!"

Today's verse doesn't tell us to give thanks *for* all circumstances but *in* all circumstances. We're not told to thank God for our hurt but to thank Him for His faithfulness through it.

If you're struggling with thankfulness amid a difficult season, I encourage you to simply thank God for being with you. Ask Him to show you His goodness in your situation, and let Him speak to your heart.

7

A Gratitude Prayer

He gives strength to the weary and increases the power of the weak.
ISAIAH 40:29

Heavenly Father, thank You for supplying the strength I need.
Thank You that I don't have to worry about the things I'm lacking,
because You are doing a work in me and through me every single day.
I am so thankful for Your grace and Your strength.
Lead me where You want me to go. I want to do Your will.
Your strength and Your grace are more than sufficient for me.
In Jesus' name, amen.

HE GIVES *strength* TO *the* WEARY & *increases* *the* *power* OF THE *weak*

ISAIAH 40:29

8

Gratitude in Faith

I remain confident of this: I will see the goodness of the LORD in the land of the living. Wait for the LORD; be strong and take heart and wait for the LORD.
PSALM 27:13–14

The Bible describes King David as a man after God's own heart (1 Samuel 13:14). God loved David, and David loved God. Throughout the book of Psalms, you can see the roller coaster of David's life as he spoke and sang through his depression, fear, gratitude, and joy.

I love how David shows his human emotions, fears, and doubts, but then comes right back and reminds himself of who God is. That, to me, is faith.

Faith is about fighting through the doubt and fear while choosing to put your trust in God. David's faith was so strong that he praised God before he got what he prayed for.

I want that kind of faith. I want to be able to thank God not only for what He has given me but for what He is going to give me.

I challenge you to pray with faith. Put your faith in God's timing. Thank God for what you are asking for, even before it happens. Waiting on the Lord does not mean waiting to thank Him.

9

What Is Hindering You?

Therefore, since we are surrounded by such a great cloud of witnesses, let
us throw off everything that hinders and the sin that so easily entangles.
And let us run with perseverance the race marked out for us.

HEBREWS 12:1

There was a time in my life when my own bitterness caused me to fall into such a dark pit of depression that I pulled away from God. I was miserable and felt alone. I could not see God's goodness, even when I tried.

Sometimes we hold on to bitterness or an unforgiving spirit, which keeps us from having a truly grateful heart. Such bitterness can lead to a huge divide in our nearness to God and our relationship with Him.

Ephesians 4:31–32 tells us to "get rid of all bitterness, rage and anger, brawling and slander, along with every form of malice. Be kind and compassionate to one another, forgiving each other, just as in Christ God forgave you."

Have you been hiding things that hinder you from drawing near to God? God has given us the authority to break those hindrances in Jesus' name! We don't have to be slaves to our hurt or our past.

Be kind,
and compassionate
to one another,
forgiving each other,
just as
in Christ GOD
forgave you.♥

EPHESIANS 4:32

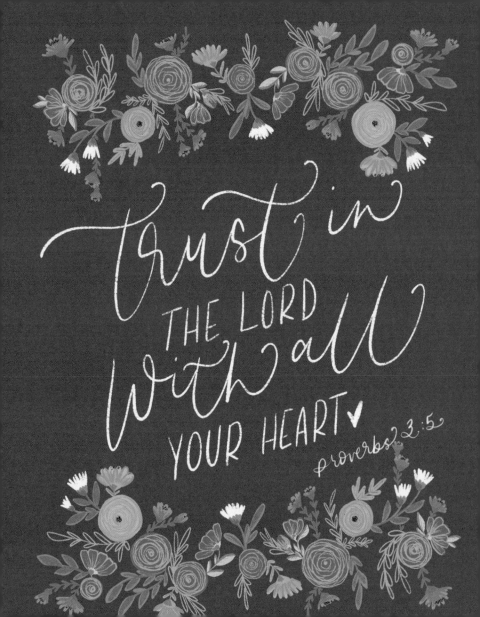

Trust in THE LORD with all YOUR HEART ♥

Proverbs 3:5

10

Acknowledging God

Trust in the LORD with all your heart, and lean not on
your own understanding; in all your ways acknowledge
Him, and He shall direct your paths.

PROVERBS 3:5–6 NKJV

Have you ever struggled with anxiety? The intrusive thoughts really take over on bad days, don't they? Thoughts like: *God doesn't care or listen to my prayers. I'm not worth a thing to anyone. I don't matter. Everything goes wrong because of me.*

It can be so easy to accept our feelings and emotions as truth. The devil loves to take advantage of times when we're struggling. He'll start to whisper lies and use our feelings to make them seem real.

This is why the Bible tells us not to lean on our own understanding. If we acknowledge God first, He will give us discernment and direction.

Part of acknowledging God is thanking and praising Him for who He is, what He has promised, and what He has done. When we take our eyes off ourselves and our situation and put them on God, we can start to see truth through the lies.

God's truth is a beautiful picture of hope, redemption, and goodness. May you rest in that thought today!

11

A Gratitude Prayer

I seek you with all my heart; do not let me stray from your commands.

PSALM 119:10

Heavenly Father, please help me let go of what hinders me.
Fill my heart with Your forgiveness and compassion instead.
Open my eyes to Your goodness as I draw near to You.
Thank You for the freedom I have in You.
Thank You for Your amazing love.
In Jesus' name, amen.

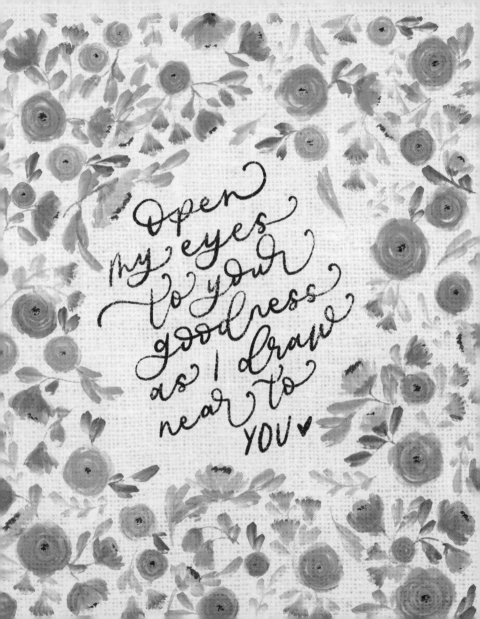

Open my eyes to your goodness as I draw near to YOU ♥

But godliness with contentment is great. gain

I TIMOTHY 6:6

12

Discontentment

Godliness with contentment is great gain. For we brought
nothing into the world, and we can take nothing out of it.
1 TIMOTHY 6:6–7

We spend so much of our time and energy on desiring, acquiring, and caring
for "things," don't we? We get stressed if our stuff gets broken or stops working. We look at the newest car, house, or gadget our friends have, and we can't
help but wish we had one too.

Discontentment is dangerous territory. It leads to greed, envy, misery,
and depression.

A grateful heart is one that is content to rest in the Lord. It learns to
recognize the blessings and trust God for its needs.

I encourage you to take some time today to search your heart for any
discontentment, jealousy, or greed. Confess it and ask God to renew your
thinking. Remind yourself that the Lord will supply your needs. Let your
heart dwell in Him.

13

What Consumes You?

Therefore, since we are receiving a kingdom that cannot be shaken, let us be thankful, and so worship God acceptably with reverence and awe, for our "God is a consuming fire."
HEBREWS 12:28–29

Back in my teen years, I was obsessed with reading and watching historical dramas. I immersed myself in my own little romance world, full of roses, libraries, ball gowns, and estates.

My interest in period dramas has stuck with me and shaped a lot of my creative style. It has influenced my love for all things flowers, my drawing and painting style, and even the colors I use.

What influences your thoughts and heart in your day-to-day life?

When we have a real relationship with God—letting Him consume our hearts and minds before anything else—He influences every aspect of our lives. It also creates a deep longing to worship and give thanks to Him, no matter what our circumstances may be.

I challenge you today to follow the Holy Spirit's prompting for worship and thanksgiving as you grow closer to God. Remember that the things of this world will never fulfill the longing for God that He has placed inside you.

Let your roots grow down into Him and let your lives be built on Him ♥

14

Deeply Rooted

Let your roots grow down into him, and let your lives be built
on him. Then your faith will grow strong in the truth you
were taught, and you will overflow with thankfulness.

COLOSSIANS 2:7 NLT

Because I live in Tornado Alley, I've seen all types of wind damage. But I have always been fascinated by the sight of trees that have been knocked over by a storm.

The roots at the base of the uprooted trees are never very long. Sometimes they're full of pests or disease. On the surface, the trees may look strong and healthy, but when their roots are put to the test, they show their weakness.

When you are tested by the storms of this life, are your roots deep and confident in the Lord's loving-kindness? We must plant ourselves in truth, with God as the foundation of our lives, so that our faith can grow and thrive.

A thriving relationship with our heavenly Father, while living in the light of His goodness, will always produce an overflow of thankfulness.

My prayer for you today is that you will examine your roots and how deep they go. Tell God about any doubts or fears limiting their depth. Ask Him to surround you with His presence.

15

A Gratitude Prayer

It is for freedom that Christ has set us free. Stand firm, then, and do not let yourselves be burdened again by a yoke of slavery.
GALATIANS 5:1

Jesus, You came to set us free by Your blood. Thank You for Your unfathomable sacrifice!

Thank You for freedom from the curse of sin and shame.

Because of You, I am made new and am no longer a slave to my old life.

Because of You, I don't have to fear the unknown. I know that I get to spend my eternity forever in Your presence.

Thank You for saving me and setting me free.

In Your name, amen.

it is for
FREEDOM
that
CHRIST
has set us
free ♥

GALATIANS 5:1

16
Thankful for the "No"

"As the heavens are higher than the earth, so are my ways higher than your ways and my thoughts than your thoughts."
ISAIAH 55:9

My four-year-old is the sweetest little girl. She has big hazel eyes and loves to do nice things for other people. She also loves chocolate and wants it every day. Sometimes I'll let her have some for dessert. Other times, though, she asks me for chocolate at bedtime and I have to tell her no.

Does saying no mean I don't love her? Absolutely not. Does she cry and tell me she thinks I don't love her? Sometimes.

What my daughter does not understand yet is that I tell her no *because* I love her and want her to be healthy. Too much caffeine and sugar can affect her little body, but she only understands that it tastes good.

How many times do we tell ourselves that God must not care about us because we don't get what we pray for?

I challenge you today to make the choice to start thanking God for both His no and His yes. We may not always understand His incredible plans, but we can trust He's always working for our good.

17

Setting the Example

Don't let anyone look down on you because you are young, but set an example for the believers in speech, in conduct, in love, in faith and in purity.
1 TIMOTHY 4:12

Have you ever been through something traumatic, only to have someone tell you to be thankful it wasn't worse? Have you ever lost a loved one and had someone point out to you that at least you still have some loved ones left? How did that make you feel?

It's so very important to remember that it is not our job to *make* someone thankful. It is not our job to point out all the things they have to be thankful for. It is our job to love others and to hold their hands while they are struggling. A grateful heart cannot be cultivated through force. It can only be influenced by our own example and encouraged through someone's own relationship with God.

If someone in your life struggles with a grateful heart, I encourage you to lift them up in prayer. Pray that God will show Himself in their life. Pray blessings on them, and keep your eyes focused on Christ.

SET AN
example
IN SPEECH,
in conduct,
IN LOVE
&
*in
purity*
1 Timothy 4:12

LORD, YOU ARE
so much better
THAN THE THINGS
of this world.

18

A Gratitude Prayer

Then Jesus declared, "I am the bread of life. Whoever comes to me will never go hungry, and whoever believes in me will never be thirsty."
JOHN 6:35

Lord, You are able to fulfill every single desire and need I have through my relationship with You.

Thank You for giving Yourself freely.

When the things of this world tempt me to pull away from You, help me remember that You are so much better than all of it!

Help me guard my heart and my thoughts when discontentment and lies start to creep in.

Keep me safely tucked away under the feathers of Your wings.

You alone are what I live for.

In Jesus' name, amen.

19

Seeking God

Don't be deceived, my dear brothers and sisters. Every good and
perfect gift is from above, coming down from the Father of the
heavenly lights, who does not change like shifting shadows.
JAMES 1:16–17

We live in a world that tells us to "look for the good" and to "think positive." We hear people we admire telling us that "mindset is everything" and
that we have the power to manifest whatever we set our minds on.

I'm here to tell you that it's a lie. And a very good plot from the Enemy
to discredit God.

If Satan can have us thinking that the blessings in our life are because
of our own doing, he can convince us that there is no need for a good and
perfect God.

I want to encourage you today to not just look for the good but to look
for the goodness of God. Being thankful is important, but if we leave God
out of it, we leave ourselves out of the truly beautiful and abundant life God
has in store for us.

GOD knows OUR needs.

20

He Knows Our Needs

In all things God works for the good of those who love him,
who have been called according to his purpose.
ROMANS 8:28

My husband and I found out we were expecting our second baby about six months before he was scheduled to be deployed overseas. At the time, the thought of taking care of a newborn and a two-year-old alone for an entire year terrified me, and I dreaded his deployment date.

I kissed my soldier goodbye when I was thirty weeks pregnant. The whole month and a half of waiting for our baby girl to arrive was a whirlwind of joy, anxiety, fear, and dread.

Finally, our daughter was born. My husband's commander sent him home on leave at the last minute, so he was able to make it in time. She was beautiful, healthy, and the best sleeper ever. After my husband went back to duty, she and her brother filled my lonely days with smiles.

God knew we needed her.

God knows your needs too. He knew them before you even came into being. Sometimes the things we receive unexpectedly turn out to be the most beautiful blessings. No matter how afraid or unprepared we may feel, when we put our trust in God's plan, we can always give thanks.

21

Contrast

I consider that our present sufferings are not worth comparing with the glory that will be revealed in us.
ROMANS 8:18

Midwest winters aren't always extremely cold, but they are usually very overcast. This past winter, the kids and I would literally start cheering whenever the sun finally showed its warmth. I'd open all the curtains, and we would curl up in the light. Even the dog would find a spot to lie in the sunshine.

It might sound odd, but I'm grateful for such gray winters because they help us appreciate the brightness of the sun that much more. If we lived in a hot, sunny climate, I don't think we would be as excited to soak it all in.

In a similar way, the darkness and grief we go through on this earth make God's glory shine all the brighter. With His strength, we can face the trials and hardships in life with gratitude—because nothing will compare to the beauty and the glory of eternal life with our heavenly Father.

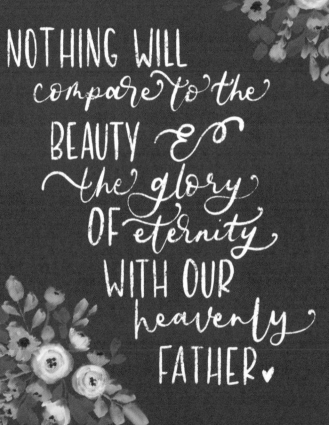

NOTHING WILL compare to the BEAUTY & the glory OF eternity WITH OUR heavenly FATHER.

Let them give
thanks to the
Lord for his
unfailing Love.

PSALM 107:8

22

A Gratitude Prayer

Let them give thanks to the LORD for his unfailing love and his wonderful deeds
for mankind, for he satisfies the thirsty and fills the hungry with good things.
PSALM 107:8–9

Heavenly Father, thank You for Your unfailing love! There is nothing I
can do to make You love me more, and there is nothing that could ever
make You love me less.

Your perfect love casts out fear—fear of rejection, fear of abandon-
ment, and fear of failure!

You accept me not because I am perfect but because through Jesus
I am made righteous. You don't see my imperfections. You only see the
blood of Jesus and Your beloved.

I love You, God!
In Jesus' name, amen.

23

Keeping Count

We are filled with the good things of your house, of your holy temple.
PSALM 65:4

One of my favorite things to do when I can't fall asleep is to pray and thank the Lord for the blessings in my life. I name each one and keep going until I run out of things to thank Him for. It almost always makes my heart calm, and I usually fall asleep before I finish praying.

There's a scripture in Joshua 12:9–24 that talks about thirty-one kings who were defeated by the Israelites. It doesn't just say "and the Israelites defeated thirty-one kings," though. The writer of Joshua wrote down each king by name and placed the word "one" next to it. By doing that, he drew attention to the many times God came through for the Israelites and how many kingdoms could not stand in the way of His plans.

Naming our blessings does the same thing as we see God working in our lives. We often lump together all the things we're thankful for, but when we take the time to name them one by one, we are also able to bring to attention God's generosity and His faithfulness over and over again.

NAMING OUR BLESSINGS
One at a time
CAN CHANGE HOW WE SEE
God working

"Never
will I leave
you;
Never
will I forsake
you."
♥ GOD

HEBREWS 13:5

24

Choosing Contentment

Keep your lives free from the love of money and be content with what you have, because God has said, "Never will I leave you; never will I forsake you."
HEBREWS 13:5

I love looking at interior design ideas. Photos of beautiful wood, walls with no crayon marks on them, and flawless white furniture make me happy and inspire me to redecorate my own home.

Sometimes, though, aspirational pictures can lead to discontentment with the present. In those moments, I don't feel grateful for what I have. I have to fight to pull my focus back to what God has already given me.

Choosing contentment and gratitude is something we must do over and over. It does not always come easily, especially when we start wanting things we don't have. Discontentment is like a pit. The further down you go, the harder it is to fight your way out.

It can be difficult to appreciate what we have when it feels like everyone else has something better than we do, but we have to remember that our purpose is greater than striving for the things of this world.

25

Surrender

Those who hope in the Lord will renew their strength. They will soar on wings like eagles; they will run and not grow weary, they will walk and not be faint.

ISAIAH 40:31

Right after I had my firstborn, I developed overwhelming anxiety. I was constantly having irrational worries about things happening to him. I also struggled with night terrors.

One day, I shared some of my fears with my mom. She listened and encouraged me, and then she reminded me of something: My son belongs to God, not me. He loves him more than I ever can, and He gives me the strength and wisdom I need to take care of him.

That piece of advice has stuck with me for the past fourteen years. When I start to question my abilities as a mother, I thank God for promising to supply what I need. Throughout the hospital stays, the medical scares, and the general struggles of raising a teenager, my son still belongs to God. I can try to control things in my own strength, or I can choose to surrender to God and lean on His supernatural strength.

My hope for you today is that you take time to reflect on what areas you might not be trusting God with. Ask Him for help in those areas, and thank Him for supplying you with the strength you need.

THANK YOU
for giving me
A LIFE more abundant
THAN I COULD
ever imagine ♥

26

A Gratitude Prayer

He will bless those who fear the LORD—small and great alike. May the LORD cause you to flourish, both you and your children. May you be blessed by the LORD, the Maker of heaven and earth.

PSALM 115:13–15

God, I bless Your holy name.

I want to love and serve You with my whole heart, soul, and mind!

Thank You for giving me a life more abundant than I could ever imagine.

Pour out Your blessings on me and my family.

I want my children and their children and the generations that follow to know and love You like I do.

Thank You for blessing us through the generations.

In Jesus' name, amen.

27

New Every Morning

The steadfast love of the LORD never ceases; his mercies never come to an end; they are new every morning; great is your faithfulness.
LAMENTATIONS 3:22–23 ESV

Do you sometimes struggle with wanting to do everything perfectly? You get up, ready to face the day with a plan, only to find yourself feeling like a failure at the end of the day because nothing happened the way you wanted it to. The entire day feels wasted, and the shortcomings seem so much more important than all the little pieces of beauty that occurred.

I still struggle with perfectionism. When anxiety kicks in, I try to remind myself that God cares more about my heart than my shortcomings and that His grace covers everything I'm insecure about. I'm so grateful God is perfect so I don't have to be.

We as sinners have absolutely no ability to be perfect, but we do have something even greater if we've accepted Jesus as our Lord and Savior: the power of Christ in us. Instead of starting a new day discouraged, we can wake up and thank Him for another beautiful morning to try again. I love that!

the steadfast love of the lord never ceases;
HIS MERCIES... ARE NEW EVERY MORNING;
great is your faithfulness ♥

NOTHING IS TOO
little for God. ♥

28

Nothing Is Too Little for God

See how the flowers of the field grow. They do not labor or spin. Yet I tell you that not even Solomon in all his splendor was dressed like one of these.
MATTHEW 6:28–29

"Thank You, God, for hot showers."

I find myself praying this so often that it makes me laugh. After a really long day, getting into the shower feels like a luxury. It's finally quiet, and I can just stand there for a few minutes and let the hot water wash away the chaos from the day.

I used to feel stupid for thanking God for something as mundane as a hot shower or a cup of coffee, but these are blessings too. God wants our gratitude for all things, little and big, because all good things are from Him. Even hot showers!

The next time you find yourself feeling silly for thanking God for something small, remember that nothing is too little for God. He wants to be acknowledged in everything, even your daily routine!

29

A God of Comfort

The LORD is close to the brokenhearted and saves those who are crushed in spirit.
PSALM 34:18

When my third baby was thirteen months old, I found out I was pregnant again. About a week later, I started to have some troubling symptoms. It was then that we found out it was an ectopic pregnancy. Not only was my left fallopian tube blocked, but there was a risk of it fatally rupturing. I was terrified.

During the drive to the hospital, God spoke to my heart and told me I was going to be okay. I remember saying, "God, I trust You," and feeling overwhelming peace wash over me. Even when I didn't understand why it had to happen, I was so thankful to know God was with me.

We may never understand some of the painful things we go through, but the Lord has promised to be our comfort. Even in our grief, we can be grateful for His loving embrace and supernatural peace. Let yourself accept that comfort with gratitude. He wants to hold our hands through the tears and grief and whisper His love and peace to our hearts.

The Lord
IS CLOSE TO THE
brokenhearted
AND SAVES THOSE
who are crushed
IN SPIRIT ♥ Psalm 34:18

BLESSED IS THE ONE
Who trusts in the LORD,
WHOSE CONFIDENCE IS IN HIM.

Jeremiah 17:7

30

A Gratitude Prayer

Blessed is the one who trusts in the LORD, whose confidence is in him.

JEREMIAH 17:7

Heavenly Father, thank You not just for the things You've already done but for the things You are doing and are going to do in my life.

Help me remember that You use every single thing that comes my way to teach me, refine me, and show Your glory through my life.

I trust You with it all!

In Jesus' name, amen.

31

Pray Always, Thank Always

Devote yourselves to prayer, being watchful and thankful.
COLOSSIANS 4:2

Not that long ago, I realized that prayer had become a to-do list item instead of a conversation with someone I loved.

I always had the best intentions to grow my prayer life. I would buy prayer journals, create lists, and tell people I was praying for them, and then I would forget to set aside time to actually pray. I knew that it was something I needed to do; I just couldn't bring myself to make the time regularly.

I started making the effort to talk to God throughout the day, and at first it was kind of awkward. As time went on, though, my prayer life started to grow. God felt real again. I could thank Him, cry to Him, and share my heart with Him, right in that very moment. I didn't have to wait to go home and pray in a quiet room.

God wants to be in your daily life too.

May you be encouraged today to pray always and bring the Lord into your daily life. He wants you to thank Him, ask Him, rant to Him, and talk to Him about all of it. He can't wait to hear from you!

devote yourselves
TO PRAYER
being watchful
AND THANKFUL ♥
colossians 4:2

THE BEST WAY TO
combat a complaining
ATTITUDE IS WITH
a thankful heart ♥

32

Attitude and Gratitude

The thief comes only to steal and kill and destroy; I have
come that they may have life, and have it to the full.
JOHN 10:10

Do you ever have days when everything seems to go wrong, no matter what you do? Maybe plans get canceled, the kids are sick, or everyone just wakes up with a bad attitude. Pretty soon you feel stuck in a downward spiral of negativity and complaining, and you become convinced there is nothing good in your day.

That is the Enemy's goal. If the devil can get you to focus on all the bad throughout your day and not find anything to be thankful for, you can't be effectively used by God.

How are we going to share the love of Christ with others if we're caught complaining all the time? How can we meet people's needs and be the hands and feet of Jesus when we are focused on ourselves?

The best way to combat a complaining attitude is with a thankful heart. We can choose to lay down our complaints and thank God for everything. Thank Him for His provision, for the air in our lungs, and for His gift of salvation.

Suddenly, those things that made our day seem so bad don't become our focus. God does.

33

A Gratitude Prayer

*Therefore God exalted him to the highest place and gave him the name
that is above every other name, that at the name of Jesus every knee
should bow, in heaven and on earth and under the earth, and every
tongue confess that Jesus Christ is Lord, to the glory of God the Father.*
PHILIPPIANS 2:9–11

Jesus, thank You that everything is made new by Your sacrifice.
Thank You that we don't have to live as prisoners of our old selves.
Your name has the power to break the chains of addiction, depression, bitterness, loneliness, and anything else we're struggling with.
Your name is above every other name.
Thank You that we can call on Your name to be saved.
I love You, Lord!
In Jesus' name, amen.

God is going to carry us through it all

34

Supernatural

Oh, taste and see that the LORD is good; blessed is the man who trusts in Him!

PSALM 34:8 NKJV

I was talking to my dad one evening after processing some really stressful circumstances. I told him that instead of panicking during that time, I immediately thanked God for certain things He had put in place before it happened. I was able to recognize God working, and all I felt was peace amid the chaos, even though others thought I was crazy.

My dad let out a chuckle and replied, "Well, it seems crazy because it's not a natural response."

He was right. A response of thanksgiving and gratitude when something bad happens isn't natural; it's supernatural. It's the peace of God and the presence of the Holy Spirit in us that cause us to be able to see the goodness of God everywhere.

When we have a relationship with God, we know He's with us and for us. We don't have to fear the future. We can lean on Him and breathe, knowing that without a doubt, God is going to carry us through it all.

35

Practice, Practice, Practice

Whatever you have learned or received or heard from me, or seen in
me—put into practice. And the God of peace will be with you.
PHILIPPIANS 4:9

When I first got into digital art, I had been doing traditional art for more than twenty years. The digital format frustrated me, and I wanted to do it perfectly right away. After struggling for a little while, I decided to draw something on my tablet every day for a whole year and document any improvements made. The progress that year in my ability to draw was incredible.

New skills and abilities take consistent practice, don't they? Developing a grateful heart does too. Our minds do not automatically switch to thankfulness mode, so we must take the time to allow our hearts and minds to be renewed daily by reading God's Word, thanking Him, and letting the Holy Spirit work in us.

I challenge you to practice thankfulness and renew your mind daily. Making those a regular part of your life can be such a blessing.

PRACTICE
gratitude
+
Renew
YOUR MIND
daily

36

All My Heart

I will thank the LORD with all my heart; I will declare all your wondrous works.
I will rejoice and boast about you; I will sing about your name, Most High.

PSALM 9:1–2 CSB

My two-year-old son is the youngest of our five kiddos. He is the type of toddler who has no medium setting. When he's happy, he's exuberant. When he's sad, he's devastated. He will climb to the very top of something before he'll even consider coming back down, and when he runs, he goes full speed.

In the book of Psalms, David says several times that he will thank the Lord with all his heart. Not just some of it. David praised God with his whole being.

Likewise, God wants all of us. Not just our Sunday best or our thanks when we get something we want. He wants an intimate relationship with us. And for our complete focus to be on Him.

I pray that today as you go about your busy schedule, you keep your focus on God and what He has done for you. Then, whatever you do, do it all for His glory.

37

A Gratitude Prayer

Let us then approach God's throne of grace with confidence, so that we may receive mercy and find grace to help us in our time of need.
HEBREWS 4:16

God, thank You that You have promised to never leave me.

Thank You that Your Spirit lives in me, guides me, and comforts me.

Thank You that through Jesus, I can approach You at any time with anything.

You love me and care about me more than I could ever comprehend.

I am so grateful for Your love!

Help me draw closer and closer to You each day.

In Jesus' name, amen.

THE LORD IS MY STRENGTH and my defense; he has become my salvation. HE IS MY GOD AND I WILL PRAISE HIM.

exodus 15:2

38

Salvation

The Lord is my strength and my defense; he has become my
salvation. He is my God, and I will praise him.
EXODUS 15:2

If you were on the brink of death, dangling from a precipice over a chasm filled with boiling lava, and suddenly someone swooped in and saved you, do you think you would be grateful?

If you were thrown into a pit full of deadly snakes with no way out, and someone threw you a rope and pulled you up, do you think you would appreciate them?

I think the majority of us would say yes to the above questions, don't you?

Now picture this: You're condemned to burn in agony forever without dying, enduring an eternal sentence full of terror and pain, with no way out. . . . Then someone takes your place so that you can go free. Would you thank that person?

Someone really did that. His name is Jesus, and He loves us that much.

Thinking about it that way makes me want to run into His arms and cry "thank You" a million times over.

39

The Peace of God

*Do not be anxious about anything, but in every situation, by
prayer and petition, with thanksgiving, present your requests to
God. And the peace of God, which transcends all understanding,
will guard your hearts and your minds in Christ Jesus.*

PHILIPPIANS 4:6–7

Do you ever panic when something stressful happens to you? Your heart
starts pounding, and it feels like the floor is going to slide out from under
you. The feeling follows you all day and all night. You can't sleep or focus on
anything else.

That type of worry consumes us by putting our focus on fear. Thanksgiving
moves our focus to God instead.

God wants us to remember that He has a plan. He wants to bestow such
a peace on us that it surpasses everyone's understanding. Through that peace,
we are able to think clearly, remember truth, and hold on to hope.

The next time trials occur, I encourage you to pray, to thank God for
His blessings, and to keep your focus on what He can do. His way is so much
better than ours!

THANK GOD
for the perfect
PART YOU PLAY
in His perfect
PLAN.

40

Renewing Your Mind

Do not conform to the pattern of this world, but be transformed
by the renewing of your mind. Then you will be able to test and
approve what God's will is—his good, pleasing and perfect will.

ROMANS 12:2

This world is always searching for more. From a young age we are taught and influenced about what will make us truly happy. We're left thinking that if we only had a different career, a bigger house, a better partner, or a nicer body, we might finally find true joy.

The patterns of this world break us and leave us empty. It's up to us to break free from those patterns and renew our minds through reading God's Word and having a strong relationship with Him.

The renewing of our minds brings transformation into our lives. It brings gratitude and contentment with the things God has given us, and it shifts our perspective to heavenly things. It reminds us that we belong to God, and it allows the Holy Spirit to show us where God wants to use us.

My prayer for you today is that you will make the choice to break free from the world's hold on you. Let God show you the beautiful purpose He has for you, and thank Him for the part you play in His perfect plan.

41

A Gratitude Prayer

*"Call to me and I will answer you and tell you great
and unsearchable things you do not know."*
JEREMIAH 33:3

Heavenly Father, I just want to know You.
    Change my heart and fill it with Your love, peace, and gratitude.
    Fill me with Your Holy Spirit.
    *Take the brokenness and the bitterness in me and heal me from the
inside out.*
    Thank You for drawing near to me. Thank You for loving me.
    Holy Spirit, speak to my heart—I'm listening!
    Thank You that You hear my prayers and You are faithful to answer.
    I love You, Father. I need You. I'm so, so grateful for You!
In Jesus' name, amen.

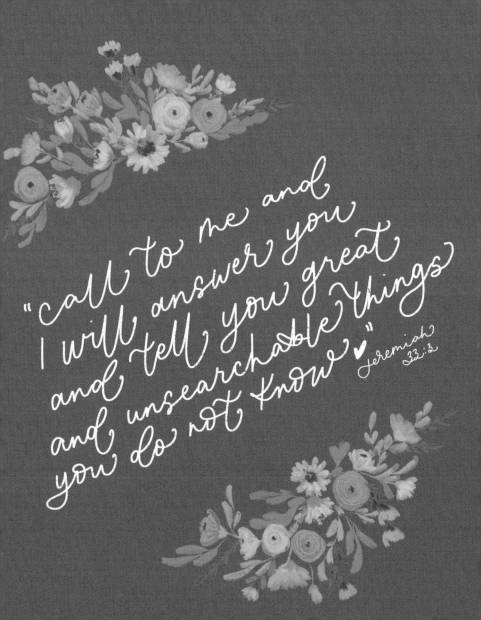

"call to me and I will answer you and tell you great and unsearchable things you do not know"

Jeremiah 33:3

LORD, REVEAL YOUR GOODNESS TO ME.

42

Ask Him

"Ask and it will be given to you; seek and you will find;
knock and the door will be opened to you."
MATTHEW 7:7

Maybe you're reading this and you're still struggling with spending time with the Lord and practicing gratitude. Perhaps you're going through a really rough season, and it doesn't seem like there's much to be thankful for.

I want you to know that it's okay. You're not alone in feeling that way.

The amazing thing about God is that He can take broken, empty vessels like us and fill them to the brim. All we need to do is ask Him. There is no one too broken or too lost to be used by God. He is the author, healer, and perfecter of our faith.

I encourage you today to ask the Lord for what you're lacking. Ask Him to move in your heart and life and to reveal His goodness. He is the true giver of all good things.

43

Worship

Come, let us bow down in worship, let us kneel before the LORD our Maker; for he is our God and we are the people of his pasture, the flock under his care.

PSALM 95:6–7

Have you ever wondered what worship is and why it's important?

Worship is coming before God in a humbled manner. It is the process of our hearts recognizing that God is first in our lives, and that nothing is more important than Him. Gratitude prepares our hearts to worship the Lord.

With grateful hearts we can see God and His glory. With grateful hearts we recognize His goodness and faithfulness.

Throughout Scripture, gratitude and worship not only moved the people's hearts toward God but moved God's heart toward His people.

May you be encouraged today to spend some time thanking and worshiping the Lord. Remember that the One who created the universe took the care to create you with a beautiful story and purpose.

with grateful
hearts we can
see GOD and His
glory

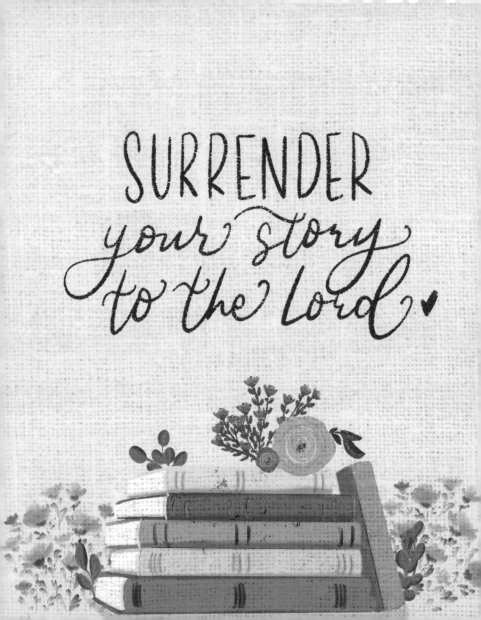

44

Hope in Your Story

*Therefore, if anyone is in Christ, the new creation has
come: The old has gone, the new is here!*
2 CORINTHIANS 5:17

Do you tend to dwell on the past? If you're like me, you may question yourself and wonder if your life today would be different if you had made better decisions.

This kind of thinking can be exhausting, but we don't have to live that way. God redeems our choices and our mistakes. Jesus didn't die on the cross so we could remain buried in our sin, hurt, and shame. He died to redeem us. To make us new in Him. Isn't that beautiful?

If I could go back in time, I would tell my younger self to hold on to Jesus—that a relationship with the Lord is so much more fulfilling than what she's ever known. But since I cannot change the past, I can rest in what God is doing and has done. From all that I've gone through, I have gained wisdom, strength, empathy, compassion, and patience. I am grateful for my story, and you can be grateful for yours too!

My hope for you today is that you hand your story to the Lord. Thank Him for redeeming every step of your journey—both yesterday and today.

45

A Gratitude Prayer

We are glad whenever we are weak but you are strong;
and our prayer is that you may be fully restored.
2 CORINTHIANS 13:9

Jesus, thank You that we don't have to struggle to do things in our own strength but that we can rely on the strength of Your Holy Spirit in us.

You don't ever make us endure anything without giving us the supernatural strength we ask for.

You know this life is hard, and You endured a human life and a horrific death to show us that.

Nothing we go through is unnoticed or hopeless. You conquered it all through Your Spirit that lives in us, and You have given us the authority to do the same.

Thank You for the gift of Your Spirit living in us.

I love You, Jesus!

In Your name, amen.

don't let others'
LACK OF FAITH AFFECT
your grateful
heart ♥

46

A Heart Full of Thanks

The LORD is my strength and my shield; my heart trusts in him, and he helps me. My heart leaps for joy, and with my song I praise him.

PSALM 28:7

You've probably heard the expression "misery loves company." Throughout life, you will meet people who want you to join in their hopelessness and who refuse to see God's goodness. To them, your hope in times of trouble is annoying or unpleasant simply because it offends their own misery.

A grateful heart is not numb to negative emotions, but it turns to God and gives thanks in the midst of those emotions. It does not pressure people to simply be positive but comforts others and encourages them in the Lord. A grateful heart sees God's goodness in spite of the chaos around it.

I'm reminded of the book of Job in the Bible. Job was a righteous man, and God allowed Satan to test him. All of Job's friends were baffled by his faith. Even his wife told him to "curse God and die" (Job 2:9). But Job loved and obeyed the Lord despite what others said, and in the end, God redeemed all he had lost.

My prayer for you today is that you hope in the Lord regardless of circumstances. Keep shining His light, and don't let others' lack of faith affect your grateful heart.

47

Perspective

The God of all grace, who called you to his eternal glory in
Christ, after you have suffered a little while, will himself
restore you and make you strong, firm and steadfast.
1 PETER 5:10

Perspective can change everything. When we grow in our relationship with the Lord, we also shift from viewing things the way we once did, and we start to see them as God wants us to. A gratitude perspective looks at things through the lens of God's goodness.

God does not cause the pain in the world; sin does. But because God is good, He can use hurt and pain to get our attention and bring us back to Him. He can use our struggles to help us learn how to lean on His supernatural strength. There is nothing He can't redeem and use for His glory.

A "me" perspective looks at things through the lens of how I'm feeling in the moment. My negative feelings and thoughts create a place for Satan to attack and drive me into depression and anger toward God.

Ask the Lord to shift your perspective to one of gratitude today. Thank Him for using all things for your good.

a gratitude perspective
LOOKS AT THINGS
through the
lens
OF GOD'S GOODNESS.

heavenly FATHER, you are so GOOD to me ♥

48

A Gratitude Prayer

This is the testimony: God has given us eternal life, and this life is in his Son.
1 JOHN 5:11

Heavenly Father, thank You that I don't have to fear the future.

You know the ending of all things, and You have already defeated death through Your Son, Jesus.

I am so grateful that I can look forward to an eternity of being in Your presence—an eternity without pain, without sorrow, and without fear.

You are so good to me!

In Jesus' name, amen.

49

God Looks at the Heart

Search me, God, and know my heart; test me and know my anxious thoughts.
See if there is any offensive way in me, and lead me in the way everlasting.
PSALM 139:23–24

My nine-year-old is the middle of our five children, and the only one who has blue eyes. Since she was a baby, her big blue eyes have given away her emotions. They sparkle when she's happy, glare when she's angry, and get very wide when she's not telling me the truth. She'll argue with me when I call her bluff, and I always tell her I know the truth because I'm her mom.

We may think we know our kids well, but our heavenly Father knows us better than anyone else on this planet. No matter how hard we may try, we cannot hide our hearts from Him. He's aware of every thought, feeling, and temptation, and He loves us regardless.

God loves us so much that He doesn't want anything to get in the way of our relationship with Him. If we are trying to hold on to sin, it can come out as ingratitude, anger, selfishness, and pride.

If any of those things are coming from your heart, it's time for a heart check. What are you trying to keep from handing over to the Lord? I encourage you to ask the Holy Spirit to show you and fill your heart with gratitude. Ask Him to help you trust in His goodness and kindness, surrendering whatever may be getting in the way of your relationship with Him.

We cannot hide our hearts from God

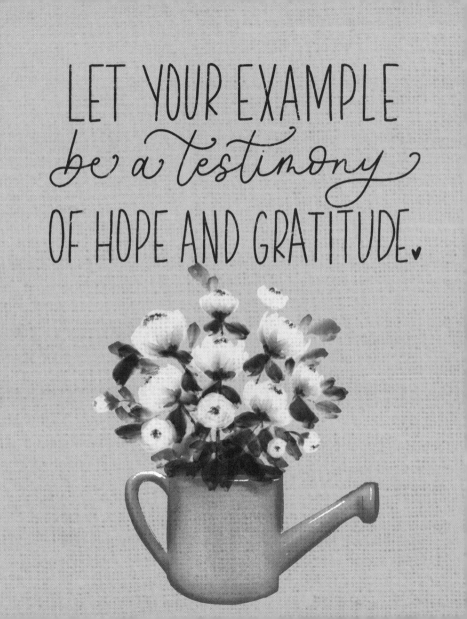

LET YOUR EXAMPLE
be a testimony
OF HOPE AND GRATITUDE.

50

Set Apart

You are a chosen people, a royal priesthood, a holy nation,
God's special possession, that you may declare the praises of him
who called you out of darkness into his wonderful light.

1 PETER 2:9

People notice things. They notice when you bow your head and pray silently over your meal at a restaurant. They notice when you stop and help someone in need. They notice when you're speaking to your children who are acting up in the middle of the store while you're on a grocery run. They also notice your response while facing hardships and trials.

Do your actions and words reflect who you belong to?

We talk about how much a grateful heart can change our own lives, but it can also change the lives of the people around us. When we respond to negative situations in a positive way, with hope in the Lord, gratitude for His goodness, and peace instead of panic, we are shining God's light out into the darkness. This is how we are supposed to live.

May the light of the Lord shine through you today, no matter what you may face. Let your example be a testimony of hope and gratitude.

51

Gratitude Is God's Will for Us

*The world and its desires pass away, but whoever
does the will of God lives forever.*

1 JOHN 2:17

When I was growing up, the church put heavy emphasis on "finding God's will" for my life. I always viewed it as some big revelation I would somehow receive. I questioned every career path and college choice as to whether it was God's will or not.

We complicate God's will so much, when the very fact of the matter is that His will for us as believers is simply to obey Him and follow His Word.

First Thessalonians 5:18 says, "Give thanks in all circumstances; for this is God's will for you in Christ Jesus."

God wants us to recognize His goodness in our lives no matter what we may be going through. He wants us to hope in Him, draw near to Him, and never let go. He wants us to know Him fully and experience all the blessings a life deeply rooted in faith can bring.

Throughout your day, may you rest in His love, give thanks for His gifts, and seek to follow His perfect will for your life.

THE WORLD AND ITS
desires pass away
BUT WHOEVER
does the will of
GOD LIVES FOREVER.

1 JOHN 2:17

thank you
THAT NOTHING I GO THROUGH
is without
purpose.

52

A Gratitude Prayer

Fear of man will prove to be a snare, but whoever trusts in the LORD is kept safe.
PROVERBS 29:25

Heavenly Father, thank You for placing me where I am right now and for giving me purpose in this moment.

Help me be content in the current circumstances while I wait on You and Your timing.

Teach me the things You want me to learn, and grow me in wisdom and in patience.

Thank You that nothing I go through is without purpose.

Help me to trust You always and to come to You with my worries first.

Thank You for never letting me down. You are so good to me! In Jesus' name, amen.

53

Gratitude Opens Doors

I, with shouts of grateful praise, will sacrifice to you. What I have vowed I will make good. I will say, "Salvation comes from the LORD." And the LORD commanded the fish, and it vomited Jonah onto dry land.

JONAH 2:9–10

There are times in life when God hears our prayers, but He is waiting for our hearts to be in line with His will before He answers.

In the Old Testament story, Jonah chose to disobey God and then run from Him. God saw Jonah's disobedience and sent a giant fish to swallow him whole after he had been thrown off a boat.

While Jonah was inside the fish, he yielded to God. He confessed and offered up a song of thanksgiving. It was then that God commanded the fish to vomit him out. Thanksgiving is a sign of a heart that is right with God. A grateful heart knows it deserves nothing but is thankful for what God has done and will do.

The act of obedience and giving thanks can open doors and move God's heart. God recognizes hidden motives, but a truly humble, grateful heart causes Him to respond.

I, WITH SHOUTS OF
grateful, praise,
WILL SACRIFICE TO YOU.

jonah 2:9

54

Whatever You Do

Whatever you do, whether in word or deed, do it all in the name of
the Lord Jesus, giving thanks to God the Father through him.
COLOSSIANS 3:17

Sometimes I let the mundane, everyday tasks get to me. Changing diapers, washing dishes, cooking meals, doing laundry, and countless other things throughout the day make it hard to be thankful. Sometimes I feel like my job as a mother is not as important as other career paths.

That is an illusion from the Enemy, who wants our joy and excitement to be found in things outside the goodness of God. He wants us to second-guess our calling, to believe the lie that where we are right now is not important.

Giving thanks for where you are *right now* changes your mindset and your motivation. It fosters peace over the discontentment you may have been feeling. A heart of gratitude takes the focus off us and puts it back on God.

I encourage you today to take a breath and thank God for where He's put you in the moment. Whether you're at work, at home, alone, or taking care of a pack of wild kiddos, you are right where you need to be.

55

The Beautiful Loop

LORD, you are my God; I will exalt you and praise your name, for in perfect faithfulness you have done wonderful things, things planned long ago.

ISAIAH 25:1

We often struggle with distractions, forgetfulness, and just plain laziness, don't we?

There have been times throughout my walk with the Lord when I have gotten out of the habit of spending daily time with Him and thanking Him for the things He has given me. Pretty soon, a couple of days turned into a couple of weeks, and before I knew it, the things coming out of my mouth and coming forth in my life were the complete opposite of what God wanted.

Practicing daily gratitude draws us closer to the Lord. It is a part of worship and praise that is essential to our relationship with Him. It's like a beautiful, perpetual loop: recognizing God's goodness, thanking Him, drawing closer, listening to what He has to say, being in awe of His goodness, and thanking Him again.

The nearer we are to Jesus, the more we crave His nearness. The more we see the goodness of God, the more we thank Him.

Make time to spend with the Lord. Let Him be the most important part of your day.

practicing DAILY *gratitude* DRAWS US *closer to* THE LORD.

THANK YOU
for being a
GOD OF
details

56

A Gratitude Prayer

I praise you because I am fearfully and wonderfully made;
your works are wonderful, I know that full well.

PSALM 139:14

God, thank You for being a God of details.

You created things both big and small, and You made each one perfectly.

There is no detail that escapes Your mind, and there is no problem You cannot solve. You are marvelous!

I look at the beauty of nature on this earth You created, and I admire Your works of art.

You created it all and said that it is good.

Thank You for letting me experience Your goodness each day.

I love You, God!

In Jesus' name, amen.

57

In His Strength

The LORD is my strength and my shield; in him my heart trusts, and I am helped; my heart exults, and with my song I give thanks to him.
PSALM 28:7 ESV

I am so thankful to know that when I don't feel strong or brave enough to face hard things alone, all I have to do is call on the Lord. Fear and worry try to convince us that we don't stand a chance, but God repeatedly tells us that He will give us what we ask for.

Psalm 28 is a song about a thankful heart that trusts in God's faithfulness. As children of God, our hearts can also trust Him to be there for us and meet our needs.

Do you struggle with worries and fears and expectations? Do you sometimes feel like you have to handle everything on your own? Let the Lord help you. He will give you what you need when you need it. All you need to do is ask Him.

THE LORD IS
my strength
and my shield;
in him my heart
TRUSTS, and I am
helped

Psalm 28:7 ESV

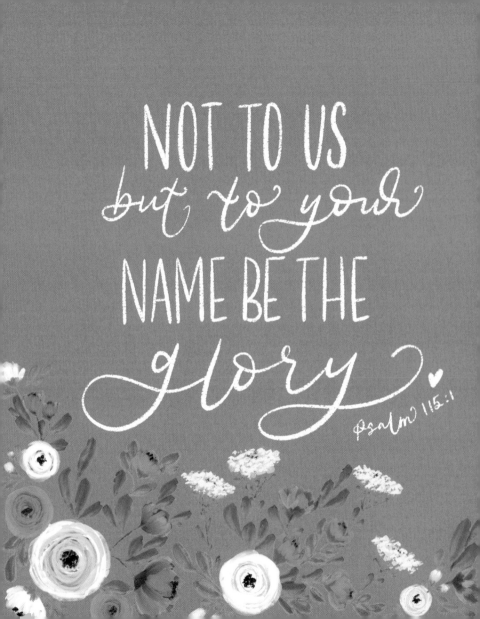

58

Where Credit Is Due

Not to us, LORD, not to us but to your name be the
glory, because of your love and faithfulness.
PSALM 115:1

How many times do we put God in a box, refusing to acknowledge anything beyond what traditions and opinions have taught us? How many times have we dismissed the beautiful mystery of God as mere coincidence? We give credit to doctors, service personnel, and leaders for the things they do, yet we often fail to acknowledge the ultimate power of the One who created and equipped them.

A grateful heart sees God behind the scenes. It acknowledges the Lord's hand in our lives and gives Him the credit. We didn't get a "lucky break," and we didn't receive blessings just because we sent something out into the universe. All that we have and all that we are is because of God's grace and through His power.

The next time something good in your life happens, I pray that you take a moment to recognize the Author of it all and express your gratitude to Him. He loves you more than you could ever know!

59

Make His Deeds Known

Oh give thanks to the LORD; call upon his name;
make known his deeds among the peoples!
1 CHRONICLES 16:8 ESV

I've made it a habit recently to thank God out loud for little things throughout the day. Before, I never really thought it was a big deal whether or not we thanked God out loud or in quiet, but I've realized that giving thanks aloud teaches my children to be grateful too.

My four-year-old and I were looking for a hair tie the other day. With three daughters, all with hair as long as my own, hair ties vanish at an astonishing rate in our home. But we found one, and as I held it up, my daugher shouted, "Yay, God! I just love God!" It was such a blessing to hear her squeaky little voice offering up praise.

I want to be a voice of praise, shouting from the rooftops about what the Lord has done for me. I want to thank Him and give Him praise in my own home without a single thought.

Next time you find yourself feeling grateful, try thanking God out loud. It may take a little while to get the hang of it, but it can be such a blessing to yourself and others around you.

OH GIVE THANKS
TO THE LORD;
CALL UPON HIS NAME;
MAKE KNOWN HIS DEEDS
AMONG THE PEOPLES.

PSALM 105:1 ESV

60

A Gratitude Prayer

God saw all that he had made, and it was very good.

GENESIS 1:31

Heavenly Father, thank You for the little things that bring me joy!

Thank You for things like a cozy day at home, the beauty of candlelight, and the fresh smell of a rainy day.

All good things come from You.

You are so wonderful.

Thank You for letting me experience beauty and goodness in this life.

Please open my eyes to Your goodness all around me, and help me share it with others in a way that glorifies You.

I love You, God!

In Jesus' name, amen.

61

God Understands

"I the LORD search the heart and examine the mind, to reward each person according to their conduct, according to what their deeds deserve."

JEREMIAH 17:10

"Trust your heart. Listen to your heart. Follow your heart."

These are things the world preaches to us every single day. They're words a lot of us have believed at one time or another.

Jeremiah 17:9 says, "The heart is deceitful above all things and beyond cure. Who can understand it?"

The answer? Only God understands the heart.

I believe God wants us to give thanks continually as a way to keep our focus on Him. When we willingly seek and build a relationship with the Lord, we're led into a life more abundant than we could ever imagine.

May you be encouraged today to lean on God and His Word, not the feelings of your heart. Practice gratitude and pursue Him with everything in you. He is calling you to Him. All you need to do is answer.

"I the LORD search the heart AND EXAMINE THE MIND❤"

Jeremiah 17:10

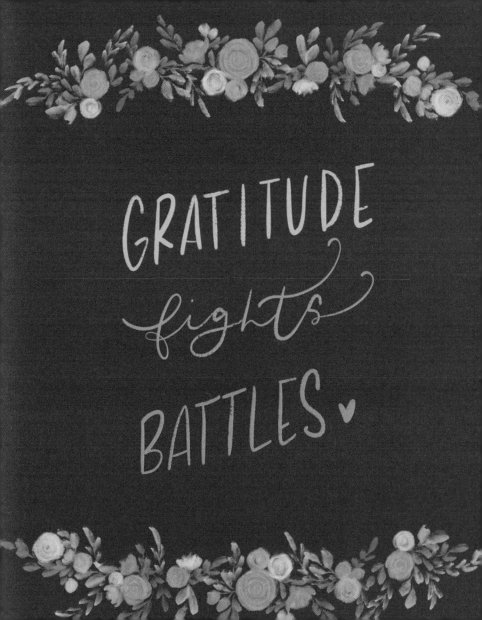

GRATITUDE

fights

BATTLES ♥

62

Gratitude Fights Battles

Though we live in the world, we do not wage war as the world does.
The weapons we fight with are not the weapons of the world. On
the contrary, they have divine power to demolish strongholds.
2 CORINTHIANS 10:3–4

Have you ever felt like you were stuck in a spiritual dry spell, and no matter how hard you tried to fight it, you couldn't help but feel ungrateful and discontented?

Friends, I'm here to tell you that the Enemy's favorite strategy is to distract you with discontentment so you begin to believe his lies. When we focus on the things we don't have, it's easy to start questioning God's plan for us. We think about our brokenness and what we're lacking instead of Jesus' redemption and blessings.

Gratitude helps us fight the spiritual battles we face by removing strongholds of bitterness, envy, anger, and strife. It puts our focus on the beautiful grace we have been given and the One who has given it.

Today, pour out your gratitude to the Lord. Let go of any strongholds you may be giving to the Enemy, and ask the Lord to renew your thinking. He's ready and waiting to draw you closer in your relationship with Him.

63

A Gratitude Prayer

Out of his fullness we have all received grace in place of grace already given.
JOHN 1:16

God, thank You for Your grace.
You are gracious, compassionate, and loving.
Thank You for wanting to bestow Your favor on us, even when we didn't deserve it.
You created this world and gave it to us to take care of.
You made a way to restore our dwelling with You.
You promise to come back for us and let us reign with You forever one day.
Your grace has no end.
I am so glad of it!
Thank You for hope and a future.
In Jesus' name, amen.

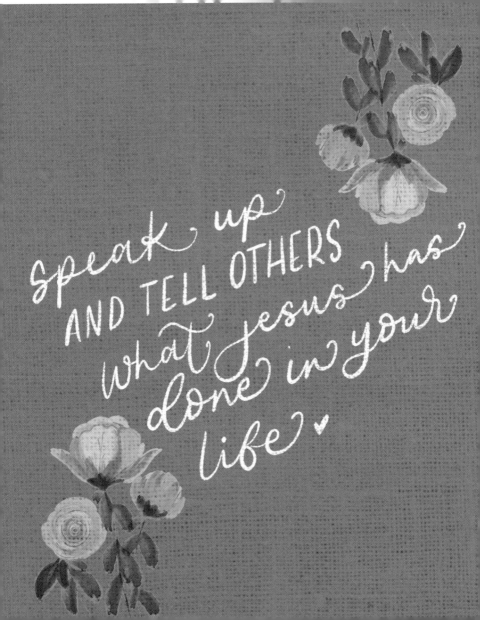

64

Contagion

[God] has committed to us the message of reconciliation. We are therefore Christ's ambassadors, as though God were making his appeal through us. We implore you on Christ's behalf: Be reconciled to God.

2 CORINTHIANS 5:19–20

One time I watched a zombie movie with my husband. The gist of the storyline was that a medical "cure" was spreading an airborne disease that wiped out most of the world. After finishing the movie, I thought about what would happen if there was actually an airborne cure for the things that make this world a fallen, dark place full of sickness and death.

Can you guess where I'm going with this?

Gratitude and excitement about the love and saving grace of Jesus can spread as intensely as a super-airborne zombie virus. People everywhere are looking for purpose in their lives that only Jesus can give.

Simply by sharing what we are grateful for and to Whom we are grateful, we are planting seeds for the kingdom of God.

I challenge you today to speak up and tell others what Jesus has done in your life. Spread the Good News as if people's lives depend upon it. Because they do.

65

Sing of His Goodness

I will sing of the LORD's great love forever; with my mouth I will make your faithfulness known through all generations.

PSALM 89:1

How many times have we been encouraged by believers and their testimonies even long after they were gone? People like Corrie ten Boom, Martin Luther, or the apostle Paul. Their faith despite their circumstances and their gratitude amid hardships have brought hope in the Lord to so many.

Your story has the potential to bless generations. Your patient gratitude and trust in the Lord during trials can influence and encourage others not only now but possibly hundreds of years from now.

We all have the opportunity to be thankful for the Lord's goodness. Expressing that gratitude and being a light to others makes it even more special. Don't ever underestimate the work the Lord can do through you.

Go out there and share your wonderful story of what God is doing in your life!

I WILL SING OF
THE LORD'S
great love
FOREVER.

Psalm 89:1

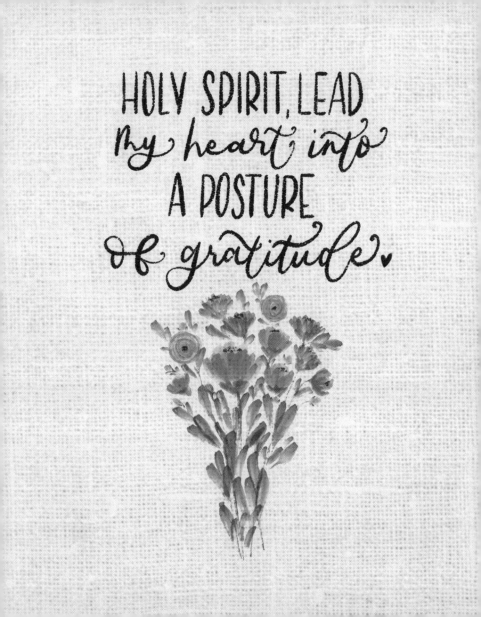

66

The Holy Spirit

"The Advocate, the Holy Spirit, whom the Father will send in my name, will teach you all things and will remind you of everything I have said to you."
JOHN 14:26

Being still can be challenging. I would be lying if I told you I didn't sometimes lock myself in the bathroom and sit on the floor by the sink to have quiet time with the Lord. It often feels like chaos starts the minute I try.

As important as it is to read our Bibles and pray, it's equally important to take time to listen to what the Holy Spirit has to say to us. Oftentimes, I am flooded with immense gratitude when I sit quietly after reading Scripture. The Holy Spirit in me prompts me to stop and notice the beautiful goodness of what God has promised us in the Bible and what He is saying to me personally.

Do you take time to listen to the Holy Spirit during your moments with the Lord? Listening to His whispers in our hearts leads us into worship and gratitude. Praying is important, but we can miss out on so much more when we don't take the time to also listen.

Be intentional about listening to what the Holy Spirit has to say. Ask Him to lead your heart into a posture of gratitude.

67

A Gratitude Prayer

God is our refuge and strength, an ever-present help in trouble.
PSALM 46:1

Heavenly Father, thank You for Your perfect peace that passes all understanding.

You are not a God of chaos and disorder, and You call us to come to You for peace and rest.

You alone are my refuge in troubled times.

Only You can calm the storms that rage inside my head.

Thank You for sending Your Spirit to live in me and minister to my soul, even when I don't have the words to pray.

You have given Your children every single good thing we need for a whole and healed life.

Please be my peace today.
In Jesus' name, amen.

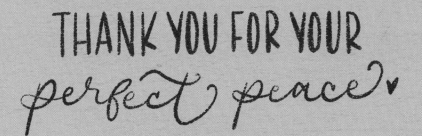

THANK YOU FOR YOUR
perfect peace

HE WHO PROMISED is faithful

HEBREWS 10:23

68

Gratitude for His Faithfulness

Let us hold unswervingly to the hope we profess, for he who promised is faithful.
HEBREWS 10:23

Was there a time in your life when someone made you a promise they could not keep? Did it affect the way you put your trust in others?

Sometimes things happen that we have no way of predicting. Even when we ourselves make a promise, we can't always control the outcome.

That's what I love about God. He is unchanging and ever-faithful. We can give thanks to Him before even asking, because we don't ever have to fear that He will fail us. Every single thing He promises, He can and will do. That is the faithfulness of our heavenly Father.

May you rest in the promises of God today and every day. May you thank Him confidently as you pour out your heart and lay your requests at His feet.

69

Redemption

In him we have redemption through his blood, the forgiveness
of sins, in accordance with the riches of God's grace.
EPHESIANS 1:7

My daughter was whining about the heat this summer and telling me how we needed to go to the public pool, even though she had just been there the day before. I raised my eyebrows and pointed to the deflated, mossy, pathetic-looking vinyl pool from last year that was still in the backyard due to rainstorms and forgetfulness.

The skeptical look my daughter gave me was priceless. Eventually, she gave in and got to work. Despite a hole that we patched, it actually cleaned up pretty well. The kids had so much fun playing in it the next day, and they kept talking about how thankful they were to have a pool again and how cool it was that we could save it.

It makes me think of redemption and how grateful I am that God made a way for us to be with Him through Jesus' blood on the cross. He could've decided to just forget it—that we weren't worth the sacrifice—but He didn't.

I pray that you rest in the beauty of redemption today, thinking about how (just like that pool) Jesus created a way for our hearts to be scrubbed clean, mended, and filled to the brim with God's grace! Thank You, Jesus!

rest in the beauty of redemption.

as we put away
things that blind us,
may the beauty of
His goodness cause
us to weep with
gratitude and joy

70

A Heart Overflowing

So then, just as you received Christ Jesus as Lord, continue to live your lives in him, rooted and built up in him, strengthened in the faith as you were taught, and overflowing with thankfulness.

COLOSSIANS 2:6–7

Before writing this devotional, I had a concern that so many words about gratitude would seem repetitive. What could I possibly write about for that many entries?

I'm so glad I listened to the Lord's calling and took up the challenge, because through it, my relationship with Him has grown immeasurably. What do I have to write about for ninety days? The same thing I will proclaim every single day for the rest of my life:

In the Lord, I have everything I need. I am moved to tears with overwhelming gratitude for the love of my Savior. The void inside me has been filled, the brokenness is being mended, and the peace that surrounds me is priceless. He has never, ever given up on me, and I never want to go back to the days when I was consumed by darkness.

I ache for everyone's eyes to be opened the way mine have been. As we put away the things that blind us, may the beauty of His goodness cause us to weep with gratitude and joy.

71

A Gratitude Prayer

*Great is his love toward us, and the faithfulness of
the LORD endures forever. Praise the LORD.*

PSALM 117:2

*Lord, when I take the time to get to know You, I can't help but love You.
You speak love and life into my soul.*

*Thank You for allowing me to approach You and to know Your
loving-kindness.*

Thank You for satisfying and filling what is missing in my heart.

*My heart overflows with love and gratitude in knowing that You
chose me and You want me.*

You are such a good Father.

I love You!

In Jesus' name, amen.

GREAT IS HIS
love
TOWARD US.
psalm 117:2

your voice
is needed in
this world

72

That They May Believe . . .

Then Jesus said, "Did I not tell you that if you
believe, you will see the glory of God?"
So they took away the stone. Then Jesus looked up and said, "Father, I thank
you that you have heard me. I knew that you always hear me, but I said this
for the benefit of the people standing here, that they may believe that you sent
me." When he had said this, Jesus called in a loud voice, "Lazarus, come out!"

JOHN 11:40–43

Lazarus and his sisters, Martha and Mary, were good friends of Jesus. The Gospel of John tells us that Lazarus got sick while Jesus was away ministering to others. Jesus traveled back to see Lazarus, but when he got there, Lazarus had already been dead for three days.

The first thing Jesus did when He arrived at His friend's tomb was to thank God out loud for hearing His prayer. He testified out loud so that others would know and believe.

We can have that same effect when we pray and thank the Lord out loud. Our words have the ability to reach others and encourage them to believe in the God who is working in our lives.

Isn't that beautiful?

May you be emboldened to live out your gratitude loudly this week, sharing your faith so that others might hear. Your voice is needed in this world!

73

Gratitude Draws Us Near to the Giver

It is by grace you have been saved, through faith—and this is not from yourselves, it is the gift of God—not by works, so that no one can boast.
EPHESIANS 2:8–10

The only Christmas gift I absolutely wanted one year was an Olympic gymnast Barbie doll. She was featured in all the toy catalogs, and her TV advertisement played during every commercial break. They were so popular that they had sold out most places. Somehow, in a world before smartphones and search engines, my mom and my grandma were able to find one for me. It was the best Christmas ever! Their labor of love and effort in finding a gift I had been begging for made me feel so special.

Think about your favorite gift for a moment. What was it? Who gave it to you?

Something about our human nature responds to receiving gifts, doesn't it? We often recognize gifts as a sign of thoughtfulness, care, and love. Receiving a gift from someone we love can produce a deep feeling of gratitude and loyalty.

In short, gratitude creates a bond between the giver and the receiver.

May you often think on the wonderful gift of grace and the One who gave this gift. You are so very loved!

GRATITUDE *creates a bond between the* GIVER & THE RECEIVER.

"TO HIM WHO KNOCKS,
the door will be
Opened."

MATTHEW 7:8

74

Seek and You Will Find

Everyone who asks receives; the one who seeks finds; and
to the one who knocks, the door will be opened.

MATTHEW 7:8

Rest. Peace. Love. Joy. Strength. Hope. Restoration. Salvation.

These are just some of the good things we are promised in the Bible. I find it interesting that when I'm lacking a lot of these things, it is during a time when I have allowed something to get in the way of my relationship with the Lord. Practicing gratitude is a way to keep our minds on the Lord.

When we ask someone we love for something we need, we don't shout it from across the room, do we? No. We approach them. And then later we thank them.

In order to receive what we need, we have to first seek after God. When we do that, we come to the realization over and over that He is all we need. He is the giver of all good things and the source of our gratitude. All we need to do is approach Him.

75

A Gratitude Prayer

*The peace of God, which transcends all understanding, will
guard your hearts and your minds in Christ Jesus.*

PHILIPPIANS 4:7

Lord, thank You for being my peace in the chaos.

    Thank You for knowing what my anxious heart needs.

    *Please help me remember that You are always working things out
for my good.*

    Thank You for only wanting amazing things for my life.

    I am so glad I don't have to stay bound by fear and worry.

    I trust You to lead me into what is best for my life.

    Thank You for Your goodness.

In Jesus' name, amen.

I WILL REMEMBER
the deeds of the LORD;
YES, I WILL REMEMBER
your miracles of long ago.
I WILL CONSIDER ALL YOUR WORKS
and meditate on all your
MIGHTY DEEDS.

psalm 77:11-12

76

Remembering His Goodness

*I will remember the deeds of the LORD; yes, I will
remember your miracles of long ago. I will consider all
your works and meditate on all your mighty deeds.*

PSALM 77:11-12

I've spent most of my life living in a rural farming community. Our road
names are numbers like 1200E and 450N. For as well as I know the area, I
go by landmarks to help me remember things. I may not always remember
which road number to turn on to, but I can sure remember to turn left at the
intersection where the tree looks like a rabbit!

Spiritual "landmarks" or specific times in your life may hold similar
significance. Maybe there was an occasion when you or a loved one experienced healing—a moment when the Lord's presence was so strong that you
knew everything was going to be okay. Or perhaps there was a time when you
received a clear answer to something you had been diligently praying about.
Whatever it may be, hold on to those moments with gratitude. Revisit them
when you are feeling discouraged.

What are some spiritual landmarks in your life? Memories of when God
worked things together for your good. Think about them and take some time
to document them. Keep them close to your heart for when you need some
encouragement.

77

Blooming

"He cuts off every branch in me that bears no fruit, while every branch that does bear fruit he prunes so that it will be even more fruitful."

JOHN 15:2

Growth. It is something we strive for, yet it doesn't always happen like we wish it would. Just like actual plants and flowers, we as Christians have the ability to bloom and grow spiritually. But just like a plant, we need storms to strengthen our stems and cause our roots to deepen in the Lord. We need living water to hydrate us, the Word of God to feed us, and the Holy Spirit's pruning to make us blossom and bear fruit.

A beautiful sign of growth is gratitude for not just the sunshine in our lives but the storms too. God doesn't always cause the storms, but He can use them to help us grow in Him. Romans 8:28 says, "We know that in all things God works for the good of those who love him." Isn't that a comforting thought?

With God as our focus, we can be confident that growth and good things will come out of whatever we may face. He wants to see us bloom!

78

A Gratitude Prayer

I will be a Father to you, and you will be my sons
and daughters, says the Lord Almighty.
2 CORINTHIANS 6:18

Heavenly Father, thank You so much for choosing me and loving me.
I am so glad I am Yours.
Thank You for sending Your Son to die so that I don't have to be
separated from You.
In Jesus I am made brand-new. I'm so grateful I don't have to live
in the shadow of my past.
Thank You for a hope and a future.
Please remind me of Your perfect love when I start to forget.
Help me keep my identity grounded in You always.
In Jesus' name, amen.

79

Your Identity in Christ

See what great love the Father has lavished on us, that we should
be called children of God! And that is what we are!

1 JOHN 3:1

I am many things. I'm a woman, daughter, sister, wife, mother, influencer, artist, and friend. While there is nothing wrong with any of those things, and I take pride in them, I have realized they do not make up my worth. My worth lies in more than my abilities and my connections. My worth lies in Christ. That is the only thing that can never change or be taken away, and it's something I will be forever grateful for!

What do you place your identity in? Your career? Your abilities? Your relationships? None of that affects the way God loves you and chose you before the foundations of the earth were laid (Ephesians 1:4). Isn't it wonderful that we don't have to be the best at everything in order to compete for God's attention? We don't have to be the most successful to earn a place in His heart.

The Lord delights in us because He created us. He wants us. He loves us. We are *His*!

That is what we should rest our identity in. We matter so much that we were worth dying for!

SEE WHAT GREAT
love
THE FATHER HAS
lavished
ON US, THAT WE
SHOULD BE CALLED
Children of
GOD.

1 JOHN 3:1

TAKE TIME TO
stop, breathe,
AND LOOK FOR
God's goodness ♥

80

Let Go

You will keep in perfect peace those whose minds
are steadfast, because they trust in you.
ISAIAH 26:3

When I look back on the earlier years of my life, a lot of the bad decisions came from a place of fear. I didn't stop to pray and earnestly seek God's thoughts, but rather I scrambled and rushed to act.

So much stress and heartache could have been avoided by simply being still and pouring out my heart to God. By letting *Him* change my heart and choosing to act from a place of gratitude and trust, that discontentment and frustration would have evaporated.

Being still doesn't mean doing nothing at all. It means to surrender and to let go. It means leaving room for God to work and to do a work in you. By submitting our plans and dreams to God, we let Him shape them into things that ultimately bless us and bless others.

Don't settle and rush for second best just because of the anxiety or discontentment you're feeling. Practice gratitude. Take time to stop, breathe, and look for God's goodness. Talk to Him about what is stressing you, and ask Him for wisdom on the situation. He promises to give us wisdom when we ask.

81

A Grateful Mother

My soul glorifies the Lord, and my spirit rejoices in God my
Savior, for he has been mindful of the humble state of his servant.
From now on all generations will call me blessed, for the Mighty
One has done great things for me—holy is his name.

LUKE 1:46–49

Most of us have heard the story. An angel appeared to a young girl named Mary, telling her not to be afraid, but that she would conceive a son. God's son. She asked how it could be, since she was a virgin. The angel told her, and she didn't laugh. She didn't scoff. She agreed. She said, "I am the Lord's servant. . . . May your word to me be fulfilled" (Luke 1:38).

Mary recognized God's blessing on her. She was *grateful* to be used by God. When I read the beginning of the book of Luke, I can just feel the beautiful servant's heart and the love for the Lord that she had.

Even in uncertain circumstances, Mary expressed gratitude and sang a song of praise to God. She saw His goodness and trusted His plan.

We can do the same, no matter what we may be walking through. God's plan is always good, because *He* is always good!

GOD'S PLAN
IS ALWAYS
GOOD,
BECAUSE HE
IS ALWAYS
GOOD.♥

82

A Gratitude Prayer

*Teach me to do your will, for you are my God; may
your good Spirit lead me on level ground.*

PSALM 143:10

*Heavenly Father, thank You for hearing my prayers and for answering
in Your perfect timing.*

You have a good plan and purpose for everything.

I submit to You and to what You decide is best for me.

*Help me to discern what Your will for me is and to listen to Your
Spirit.*

*Wherever You want to send me, whatever You will have me do, I
want to do it.*

I trust in Your goodness.

In Jesus' name, amen.

83

And All These Things Will
Be Added unto You . . .

Seek first his kingdom and his righteousness, and all these things will be
given to you as well. Therefore do not worry about tomorrow, for tomorrow
will worry about itself. Each day has enough trouble of its own.
MATTHEW 6:33–34

It's so easy to get stressed out and caught up in our to-do lists, our jobs, and
the chaos of life, isn't it? Being an adult is *hard*!

Jesus understood the many burdens of living. In Matthew 6:31, He
taught that we shouldn't be consumed by worry for the next meal or the next
paycheck. Instead, we are to seek God and His kingdom first. When we put
our relationship with God first, before everything else, it not only grounds
our faith and trust in the Lord, but it also lets Him lead us into what is best for
us! The focus of things shifts. We are grateful for the things we have instead
of worrying about what we don't have.

It's so much simpler than our minds tell us!

I pray that you let the Lord lead you into His very best for your life.
Nurture your relationship with Him above everything else. Notice the dif-
ference it makes in your heart and mind.

GROW CONTENTMENT
by planting
SEEDS OF GRATITUDE.

84

Lies from the Enemy

See to it that no one falls short of the grace of God and that no bitter root grows up to cause trouble and defile many.

HEBREWS 12:15

Have you ever been close friends with a person who seems to complain non-stop? I'm not necessarily talking about somebody mean or annoying, but someone who seems to be blinded to the blessings around them. How did it affect you?

Throughout my life I have encountered many friends of this type. As an encourager, I would try to get them to see the good, but ultimately it seemed to affect me negatively. Being around it so often sucked me into a pit of complaining, discontentment, and bitterness.

Job from the Bible experienced something similar. Although he was being attacked directly by Satan, his friends and family were the ones speaking words of discouragement and doubt to him. Wisely, Job did not fall into the trap.

Lies do not always come directly from the mouth of Satan. If he can get into our ears and sow seeds of discontentment and bitterness via someone close to us, he can get us to start doubting God's goodness. Once that doubt sets in, we can't help but be affected.

My prayer for you today is that you stop listening to lies from the Enemy. Fight those seeds of complaining by planting seeds of gratitude!

85

A Life in Communion with God

"I am the vine; you are the branches. If you remain in me and I in you, you will bear much fruit; apart from me you can do nothing."
JOHN 15:5

Through all of our discussion about having a life and a heart full of gratitude, the one thing I want you to remember is that *true* gratitude comes from a life of truly knowing God.

Anyone can learn to have a thankful mindset and to be grateful for what they have. But when you actually know God and have an intimate relationship with Him, He changes your heart in addition to your mindset. A life of gratitude comes from the change on the inside of us, regardless of the circumstances outside of us.

The only way we can receive that change is by spending time in the presence of God through prayer, worship, and reading His Word. I encourage you to take the time to get to know God, not just learn about Him. Let His Spirit speak to your heart. Listen to what He has to tell you. I promise, it will change not only your mindset, but your heart and your life too!

TRUE GRATITUDE
comes from a heart that
TRULY KNOWS GOD.

I'm so grateful
you haven't
given up on
me ♥

86

A Gratitude Prayer

In God, whose word I praise, in the LORD, whose word I praise—
in God I trust and am not afraid. What can man do to me?
PSALM 56:10–11

Lord, thank You for going before me and fighting my battles.
Thank You that I don't have to fear what anyone can do to me,
because You are with me.
You have never left me, even when I didn't acknowledge Your
presence.
I'm so grateful You haven't given up on me!
You are so good and faithful to me, always.
Help me be bold in sharing Your goodness and truth with others.
I want to be a light for You!
In Jesus' name, amen.

87

Worthy

There is no fear in love. But perfect love drives out fear, because fear has to do with punishment. The one who fears is not made perfect in love.

1 JOHN 4:18

Have you ever thought that you had to be perfectly grateful or God might take away what you have? Have you ever felt like you had to quickly confess when you messed up or God might punish or withhold His blessing from you?

I used to think that because I didn't read my Bible regularly, I wasn't worthy enough to come to God in prayer. I set an impossible standard of things I had to do to gain favor in God's eyes, when in reality, I had no desire to even read my Bible because I didn't truly *know* God or spend time with Him.

I soon realized that the more time I spent just talking to God and listening to the Holy Spirit, the more I actually started to realize His immense love for me. I started to crave His Word because I craved more of Him.

All God wants from you is *you*. Not your perfection, not your list of good deeds—just you. Let that sink in and fill you with intense gratitude. The Creator of the universe *loves* you perfectly.

perfect
LOVE
drives out
fear.

1 JOHN 4:18

88

God's Promises

God is not human, that he should lie, not a human being, that he should change his mind. Does he speak and then not act? Does he promise and not fulfill?

NUMBERS 23:19

There are estimated to be over eight thousand promises from God recorded in the Bible.

The number of times God has broken one of those promises is *zero*.

Think about that for a minute. The God of the entire universe has never broken a promise. He has never gone back on His word—all throughout history. He is the same yesterday, today, and tomorrow.

That means that the things we praise Him for—His kindness, mercy, love, faithfulness, and power—will never *not* be worthy of praise and thanksgiving. God's goodness never changes, despite the fact our circumstances and emotions do.

He doesn't change His mind one day to the next. He doesn't trick us into anything. He is perfect, trustworthy, and just. And He's proved it since the beginning of time.

Thank You, God, for keeping Your promises!

89

Restoration

God demonstrates his own love for us in this: While
we were still sinners, Christ died for us.
ROMANS 5:8

We were created to be with God. To walk with Him. To talk to Him. To intimately know and love Him. When Adam and Eve disobeyed God and ate the fruit of the tree that God had forbidden them to eat from, that sin drove them from God's presence. The beautiful, close relationship they had had with Him was forever changed.

That must have broken God's heart. Even though He loved His creation, their sin and brokenness could not withstand the glory of His presence.

At that moment, God could have wiped out His entire creation and started over, but you know what? He still had love for them. He also has love for us. Before He even created the world, He knew who we were going to be and what our purpose was—and He *loved* us. He had a plan to wipe the slate clean and restore a way for us to be with Him and in His presence always.

Because of Jesus' sacrifice and His gift of salvation and redemption, if we accept it, we are immediately welcomed into the family of God with open arms. Our eternity of being in His presence and walking with Him starts at the very moment we accept Jesus as our Savior.

Thank You, Jesus, for the ultimate gift we can never repay! Your sacrifice deserves every ounce of gratitude in us! May we never take You for granted.

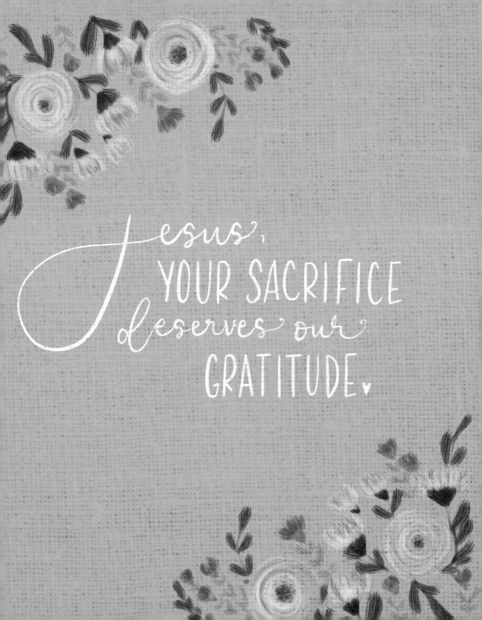

Jesus, YOUR SACRIFICE *deserves our* GRATITUDE.

90

A Gratitude Prayer

When the kindness and love of God our Savior appeared, he saved us, not because of righteous things we had done, but because of his mercy. He saved us through the washing of rebirth and renewal by the Holy Spirit, whom he poured out on us generously through Jesus Christ our Savior, so that, having been justified by his grace, we might become heirs having the hope of eternal life.

TITUS 3:4–7

Jesus, thank You that I can cast all my worries and anxiety on You instead of carrying them all.

Thank You for making my burdens light.

I don't have to wait to die to myself.

In You, I can be made new now.

Please help me remember to leave my old self and old ways at the cross.

In You, Jesus, I am made righteous.

I cannot earn salvation, but I can accept it from You.

In You, I am washed clean.

Thank You, Jesus, for Your blood that saves me!

In Your name, amen.

Acknowledgments

I would like to thank:

My husband, Brian, for supporting my gifts and abilities and for encouraging me to take a leap of faith in trying something new. I love you more than words can say!

My kiddos, Logan, Lyla, Lena, Lindley, and Lincoln, for putting up with my busy schedule and for being proud of me. You are all such blessings from God. I love you!

My parents, Dave and Kim Senseney, for their prayers and encouragement, for helping so much with my kiddos during the writing process, and for giving me a wonderful education growing up. I love you both so much!

My siblings, Jenny and Doug Walk, Joe and Alyssa Senseney, and Steve Senseney, for covering me in prayer and encouragement during this season of writing and brainstorming. I'm so thankful for each of you and for how much our friendship has grown. I love you guys!

My sister-in-law and best friend, Alyssa Senseney. You inspire me so much in both your creative talents and your walk with the Lord. Thank you for taking the time to mentor me, intercede for me, and be a listening ear! I love you!

My mother-in-law, Tina Shannon, for always being an encouragement and inspiration to me as both an artist and a mother. I love you, and I'm thankful I get to be your daughter!

My Grandma and Grandpa Waites for praying for me relentlessly and cheering for me behind the scenes. I miss you and love you so very much!

My Aunt Susie Dehmel, for praying for me and sending encouraging words when I really needed them. I love you and miss you!

My Grandma Senseney, for always encouraging my art. I wish you could be here on this side of heaven to see this book happen.

My beautiful friends—Courtney Barrett, Sarah Laswell, and Sarah Kauffman—for cheering me on, fighting for me spiritually, and encouraging me in the Lord. You ladies are such blessings in my life!

Acquisitions Editor Kara Mannix, for being so gracious and encouraging throughout this entire writing process. You are such a rare gem! I'm so glad I got to work with you!

Senior Editor Kristen Parrish, Senior Art Director Tiffany Forrester, and the rest of the team that helped this book happen. Thank you for your time and skills!

About the Author

Becky Shannon is an artist and painter who specializes in digital illustration and hand lettering. Through her business, Becky Shannon Designs, and her inspiring and art-filled Instagram account, she loves to encourage women and share the love of Jesus. A mother of five and a veteran's wife, she and her family live in central Illinois.